This is for my two beautiful butterflies
may you freely fly in the light of the Son

iii

May this book find those who are seeking comfort, reassurance, and empathy during difficult times.

"As the mother of a daughter and son-in-law who walked this painful journey of loss with miscarriage and doubts with infertility, this book allowed me to understand the pain and grief they were going through during this time. The author paints a raw, true picture of what a couple experiences during miscarriage and infertility. This book is a must read for any person, couple, or loved one who is suffering this path. And a reminder that **you are not alone.**" — J. McDaniel

"In *Conversations with Miscarriage: A Candid Journey with Pain, Grief, and Faith in the Midst of Infertility*, Marston provides a vulnerable and honest look into the minds of those going through infertility and pregnancy loss that helps others feel seen in their own journey with grief and hardship. This book is a must read for those who are experiencing loss and those who are seeking to better sympathize with those who are hurting." — **Kiera Smith**

"This is a profoundly moving book with the author sharing her raw emotions, her faith and her journey that will help you realize that you are not alone and that there is hope after miscarriage. I have never related to something I read more in my life and wish I had this book years ago when I experienced multiple miscarriages. Also a great resource book for family and friends to support loved ones suffering through the heartbreak and pain of infertility and pregnancy loss." — **Michelle Anderson**

"**A raw, gripping, honest memoir of miscarriage and infertility**. This is a must-read for anyone facing loss. Marston gives her reader permission to say the things reserved for the dark and hidden places. She writes with raw emotion and glimmers of hope. It is ultimately a message in the fight to reclaim one's faith." — **Kimberley Simms**

A Note from A.L

There are no real instructions to this piece.

It is structured as a 14-part devotional, memoir, prompt... however you'd like to look at it. You can read at your own pace. You can come back to chapters that are especially poignant to you. You can bounce around and do not have to read in chronological order.

Read and feel related to, that's the goal.

And if you feel so inspired, you can write after each chapter how the words and topic resonates with you. There is space held for you. You could write how my experience helps, how it hurts, or just how it is. This book is meant to help, and that means using it however you deem fit.

You are loved, loved, loved, my dear.

The Table of Fourteen Sometimes

The Table of Fourteen Sometimes

Foreword

I started writing this book and felt like a cliche.

It seemed that most women write about their experience with miscarriage in order to cope with its devastating loss and toll. And it certainly delivers a devastating loss and toll. It takes a toll on your positivity, your faith, your marriage, all your relationships, your physical health. So how does one cope with that? How does one say I suffered all this for...? It felt like the fill in the blank for some women was "write a book." Ding, ding, ding! You are correct, let me package up my tragic story with its happy ending in a book for the masses of tear-stained women to read.

To be fair, several of these books and devotionals truly did help me. They gave me strength and something to relate to when I felt I had neither. They provided perspective that I wouldn't have gained on my own. They even gently nudged at some medical advice that sparked conversation with my physicians. But what none of them could offer me was a pure comparison of the feelings I was having without knowing what my happy ending, my rainbow baby, my complete family looks like. All the books and devotionals I was gifted or lent or bought had their dark, tragic, soul-crushing experiences covered up in the glorious wrapping paper of several rainbow babies, biological children, a beautiful adoption, fostering forever. I do not know what that looks like for me and there is no way for me to will that into existence, trust me I've tried.

Now look, I was and am happy for these women and their families, and I was happy to hear the advice they had to share. But where was my fellow woman, broken, battered, and shattered? Did she feel the absolute chaos of emotion I felt? Did she question everything all the time as I was? Did she so desperately yearn for a glimpse of what her forever family might look like, similar to how I have tried picturing mine constantly? Insert me. If you're out there raising your hand yes to all the above, please know I am too. I sit at my dining table, having just gotten my period again and ugly cried on the floor for 20 minutes. I say, hey why not write some of this down, someone else may want to hear this. Because I know I would like to hear it.

As humans we attach story to facts or events. It is a positively human trait. Our brain fills in gaps to create a narrative. That's how we make sense of our world and process the experiences happening all around us. I think what is so difficult about being in the midst of miscarriage, is we created a story, a narrative, a happy ending that all the sudden is so violently ripped from us. Not only is our original story gone, but we stumble in attempting to create a new story. How do we attach a narrative to loss? Loss feels finite.

Something was present, and now it is gone. How do you write a story after *The End*?

1

There is the smallest seed of hope, in the smallest corner of my brain, that faintly reminds me this is not my ending, this is the not the whole story, this isn't the final plan.

I know that is the case for you too.

Wherever you are in your fertility, conception, or family planning journey, it is not the end. And while I don't feel the words I am about to type, I know that they are true: God is not finished with his plan for you or for me. "'For I know the plans I have for you,' declares the Lord, 'plans to prosper you and not to harm you, plans to give you hope and a future" (Jeremiah 29:11 NIV). I cling to those words. I clung to them in my second pregnancy. I actually wrote the following on a sticky note and hung it to my mirror: "For I know the plans I have for you to get pregnant declares the Lord. Plans to prosper you with a baby and not harm you with another miscarriage. Plans to give you hope and a future family." And guess what? I lost that pregnancy too. But just because I tried to change the plans God had for me, it didn't mean He had lost sight of whatever beautiful, heart breaking, inspiring, and painful journey He had designed for me and my eventual family here on earth.

I don't know what your future looks like dear girl, and I can't tell you what mine is. So I wrote these feelings down to help you not feel so alone. There are hundreds upon thousands of women feeling the same. They don't know what their family is going to look like but they know they so desperately want it. I knew at age 27 I was "ready" to start planning for a family. My husband and I went the old-fashioned route, lots of sex and little worry. After about 8 months without success, we begin getting frustrated and decided to be a bit more intentional and speak with our physician. That month she started running some bloodwork, and before we even got the results back, look at that! I'm pregnant! Yippee, problem solved, I just needed to get my mind off it, as they say. A week later, I suffered a threatened miscarriage, two weeks after that, an incomplete miscarriage. After my D&C procedure, I did not process well. Instead, I was ready to just jump back onto the baby making train.

During the course of very intentionally trying again for 5 months, three of my closest friends found out they were pregnant. Cue the most polarizing dichotomy of emotions I have ever experienced. That was it, time to go to the fertility doctor. Two days before the appointment... I'm pregnant! Ok I get it, now this was it. I had suffered, and now I had persevered. This was the pregnancy that was meant to be, that I deserved. At 9 and 1/2 weeks I felt moderate cramping and went in for a checkup where I felt I would be reassured all was fine. Instead, I heard the worst words I could imagine, the four little words that broke me

"There is no heartbeat."

I have started writing this 2 and 1/2 months after my second D&C.

So, I write for myself, I write for my babies in heaven, I write for my friends who have suffered the same loss, and I write for the women who intimately know this heartbreak. I am genuine, and I am brash at times, but it is all one hundred percent truly how I am feeling. I'm leaving it all on the table. If you need someone to loosely echo the gruesome and confusing ups and downs of what you've been feeling, this is for you. I have felt and experienced such a wide chasm of emotions that I sometimes get lost in the midst. I wrote them down to separate them, to examine them, and in some cases, put them behind as they do not serve any benefit to my wellbeing or the wellbeing of others. There is no chronological order to read these in, and sometimes you may be feeling them as a repeated emotion and need to read the chapter over and over.

My purpose is to love you through this book and remind you that you are not alone.
I feel this currently, I feel this every day, and I know we can get through this together.

This is a sacred space where your reflections,

pain, grief and joys are held with grace

_____

_____

_____

_____

_____

_____

_____

_____

_____

_____

_____

_____

_____

_____

_____

_____

_____

_____

_____

_____

_____

Sometimes #1

Sometimes I Feel Like I'm Fine When Everything Is Not Fine

I have my new mask on: smiling face, kind eyes, listening intently to a patient telling me about their new grandchild being born.
I'm fine.

There is no pained, forced smile or tears behind dry eyes or incessant biting of my lip. I tell myself I can go to baby showers! You are a rockstar, girl, you got this. The little truth teller that I've thrown a blanket over in the back of my mind has a look of skepticism and worry on her face. Girl, you most definitely do not got this. My husband annoyingly mirrors her sassy little honest attitude. "I don't think you're okay," he gently tells me. What do they know?

I tell myself it was one miscarriage. It is sad, and I am very upset but no more of this funny business. Let's research the excitement out of sex, and let's learn the worst out of conception, and then easy-peasy lemon squeezy. We can make this baby thing happen. Plenty of women do it all the time. They have no problems. We can will this into existence. I am fine. Truth teller rolls her eyes at me.

A few friends get pregnant and I don't? I'm still fine. Truth teller takes my hand sympathetically and looks at me doubtfully, but this is about statistics. We will make it through this. I have to persevere and work hard, and I will get my reward on the other side. Maybe we'll go to a fertility doctor just to be safe. Everyone gets easily annoyed with those they love right? Everyone wants to stay in the house and not do much right? Everyone has a deep sinking pit inside their stomach, right?

And then all those thoughts and feelings are muffled for a bit because I'm pregnant again! I am most definitely fine. Yes, I have crippling anxiety that my story will be the same round two but no, I don't need a therapist, I don't need to meditate. Maybe I'm not fine? Truth teller looks up and nods emphatically. She's saying, Let's address this! I push the thought out and just focus on the fact that I'm pregnant. But I'm learning that does not make everything fine. That does not make the anxiety disappear. In fact, it just gives way to more concern. What if I miscarry in my second trimester this time? What if I stop feeling him or her move in my third? What about when he or she is born? The anxiety spiral is endless and magnetic.

I want to scream out I am fine! But it has a little less gumption behind it, some of the confidence is wavering. Truth teller is worried, should I be worried? But I want everything to be fine. No more of this long long-suffering. Maybe I'm not actually fine but if I fake it enough, perhaps I'll start to genuinely, truly feel it. Because I don't want to keep feeling not fine. I want the two to coincide - I feel fine and everything is fine. I'm so desperate for normalcy, for peace, for just okay, that I'm willing to pretend to have it. The problem with pretending is that it doesn't seem to last. It's a tough charade to keep up.

I experience my second miscarriage. My worst fear comes to fruition. I go to counseling, I meditate, I read books, I exercise, I eat healthy. I do the things that people tell me will help me feel fine. I keep with it, but I'm not feeling it. Truth teller sees me, she tried to tell me. There's no I told you so attitude though. She takes up a bigger room in my mind now, and she's looking at my soul. She speaks my truth aloud, "you do not feel fine." I tell my husband I'm ready to go to heaven to be with our babies... I am definitely not fine.

This is a sacred space where your reflections, pain, grief and joys are held with grace

_____
_____
_____
_____
_____
_____
_____
_____
_____
_____
_____
_____
_____
_____
_____
_____
_____
_____

Sometimes #2

Sometimes I Feel Like I'm Drowning in Jealousy

Sometimes I feel like the only thing I can actually feel is envy.

This is one of the hardest feelings because this is not my personality. I don't like looking at others and coveting what they have. What's even more challenging is not only do I so intensely covet what they have, I have to secretly covet. No one likes a bitter infertile woman, I tell myself. I have to hide this ugly monster of jealousy that lives in my innermost being. I see a growing belly and scream silently but in my head it is so, so loud and deafening. In fact, it's so loud, it is the only thing I hear. I never noticed this many pregnant women before, it feels like they are everywhere I go... the grocery line, at a nice dinner, in line at the bank. My mind endlessly repeats why not me and why her? What did I do? Because I'll change it. I plead with God, I'll change anything.

I'll do anything.

A close friend of mine is pregnant. She simultaneously gets diagnosed with cancer, must undergo surgery and is in tremendous pain. I tell God, sign me up for that. I will take the pain, I will take the cancer, I will take that unknown just to be pregnant. Is that what it takes to get pregnant and have a baby? That's how I desperate I am that I am willing to have cancer, and it only further facilitates me asking myself what is wrong with me?

It's been 11 months since my first lost pregnancy and I have had 6 friends become pregnant. Six that get to announce their happy pregnancy photos with due dates, and wear cute shirts, and post bump updates. I can't even go on social media. That number will just quadruple and send me spiraling. I have never felt so isolated or alone in my life. Out of all my friends I keep in contact with, I spend time with, I socialize with regularly, I have two that do not have infants or are not pregnant. Where does that leave me? Behind, that's where it leaves me. And I go back to the simple fact that I so desperately want to be a mom here on earth.

My jealousy is eating me alive, it keeps snacking on my happiness, on my peace, and it spits back out anxiety and resentment. I am being transformed in the worst way possible. My best friend tells me she is pregnant, they weren't trying, she is nervous to tell me. I hug her tightly, and I shove, no hammer, the feeling of panic bubbling up in my chest.

"I am so happy for you!"

(I half lie.)

"How are you feeling?"

(How did this happen?)

"I am so excited for you guys."

(I don't know how much longer I can keep this smile plastered on my face until I burst into a mix of happy and sad tears.)

"This is a miracle!"

(I want this to be my miracle, too!)

They leave, and I feel my legs collapse. I'm on the kitchen floor, the tears are uncontrollable, the desperation is suffocating, I am drowning in jealousy. I plead with my husband "I am NOT strong enough to do this." I can't breathe, and all I know is I never want to feel this way again but I will several times, and I learn you cannot hammer it down and you cannot let it consume you. I find outlets, I speak my truths in counseling, and I work on getting to a place where I am simply floating in jealousy, not drowning, and I find I am strong enough to endure that.

This is a sacred space where your reflections,
pain, grief and joys are held with grace

_____
_____
_____
_____
_____
_____
_____
_____
_____
_____
_____
_____
_____
_____
_____
_____
_____
_____
_____
_____

Sometimes #3

Sometimes I Feel Like My Marriage is Falling Apart

Sometimes I feel like my marriage is falling apart, and I will never get my old husband back. Will he ever get his wife back?

We've been in survival mode for so long that it's almost like we lost what our marriage is apart from trying to conceive. It's truly all consuming, I suspect others can relate. We were once the life of the party, outgoing and happy and goofy. Now, there is no spontaneity or light heartedness left. Everything is charred and tinged with the smoke of our losses, the destruction of our deepest desires that are continually left unmet. We keep living our lives with this cloud of distraught over our heads.

Sometimes it's silent and just permeates our moods, and sometimes it's vocal and creeps out through angry tears and exasperated arguments. But regardless, this negatively charged energy is always with us. It is hard to live life with the strongest want you've ever had being ripped away from you and then continually not returned. For the first time, I'm processing this feeling of instability in my marriage. I should consider myself lucky that this is the first time I've felt a shaking in our marriage. But it is hard to ever consider yourself lucky in this situation.

And where do I begin with sex? Now I have a very complicated relationship with sex. I used to love sex, loved initiating it, loved being carefree and just enjoying this part of our marriage. But now even when I know there's no chance of being able to conceive, it's in the back of my mind. Literally I am thinking of a sperm traveling inside me to meet an egg. I'm practically willing it to happen. Sometimes we say we're taking a break from trying but I know in the back of our minds we've tracked my cycle subconsciously enough to know when I could potentially be ovulating. So even when we're "not trying," we're actually trying and of course, we never stop hoping.

Sometimes it's hard to be happy with anyone and anything, including my husband. I hate this feeling, it's not angry and it's not sad. It is the void, the absence of happiness. It is in the inability to experience happiness with another. A vacuum came and sucked all the happiness out of our home. I'll find myself just stopped in the middle of a room, looking around, where did all the happiness go? I want it back! I scream in my head. The pictures from our wedding are big and beautiful up on the walls of our home. I look at those happy, smiling, stupid, unsuspecting faces with contempt. Or maybe it's with jealousy.

The unknown of who we are becoming individually and as a couple is daunting. Will we always have this undercurrent of sadness? Or will we allow this sadness to propel our relationship into something more complex with a stronger foundation?

This is a sacred space where your reflections, pain, grief and joys are held with grace

_____
_____
_____
_____
_____
_____
_____
_____
_____
_____
_____
_____
_____
_____
_____
_____
_____
_____

Sometimes #4

Sometimes I Feel Like Everything Is Going to Be Okay

Sometimes I feel that slowly- very slowly- this broken, shattered body, heart, and mind are healing.

I sit outside in my backyard, there's a breeze and the faintest smell of salt from the ocean spray. My neighbor's windchime dings, and it's still dewy from the morning. It feels nice, and I haven't felt nice in a long time. Sometimes I feel like everything is going to be okay. The world keeps turning, it keeps rotating, and each day it turns into something new. That is what I feel like today. I am turning into something new, something resembling fine and okay. I do not want to be just fine or okay forever, but I know that will turn into something better and I sure as hell know it's better than where I've been. I would call this healing.

Slowly- very slowly- this broken, shattered body, heart, and mind are healing.

There is a peace and contentment in my heart. "I know what it is to be in need, and I know what it is to have plenty. I have learned the secret of being content in any and every situation, whether well fed or hungry, whether living in plenty or in want" Philippians 4:11-13. That verse resonates with me today. I have had highs, and I have certainly had lows, and I've come out either side knowing everything is going to be okay. Even with the highs, I recognize I will experience the elation and then it will end. That is the cycle of this life on earth.

I remember being long distance with my husband when we were dating. I would begin the drive down for the weekend to see him, radiating excitement, giddy with butterflies from early love. I was preparing for a high, a weekend of beyond just okay and fine, of frankly some of the happiest moments of my life thus far. But I also knew that 48 or 72 hours later I would be making the same drive but in the opposite direction, and I would have experienced that high and it would be done, finished. What was something initially so tangible, so anticipated, would have happened, no longer graspable or on the horizon. I would have lived a lovely, beautiful weekend, and then that would be it, done. Snap, just like that. Now hear me out, I know that may sound pessimistic but, in my mind, it's more a mindfulness technique. It's living in the true essence of the moment. It's realizing that the moment you are in does not last forever and it does not define your forever. Not that the drive back would be bad or sad or negative, it would just be. It would no longer be the excitement that I was prepared to experience beforehand.

Now I try to put that same technique into practice in the darkest moments of my life. I am living through the sinking pit in my stomach, radiating desperation, preparing for absolute exhaustion. But I can also recognize that later (maybe longer than 48 or 72 hours later), I will have experienced those feelings and this enduring situation, and I will be on the other side of it. I will be driving the same road, but these moments will be in my rearview mirror. And that realization right there allows me to feel like everything is going to be okay.

I have glimpses, hours, and occasionally days, where sometimes I feel like everything is going to be okay. I recognize that God is my portion and my prize (Psalms 16:5). These moments here on earth are temporary. The highs will come and be amazing, but they will go. The lows will sink in and be awful, but they will go. But God will remain forever, he is my forever, and he has destined for me to be okay. "*I have told you these things, so that in me you may have peace. In this world you will have trouble. But take heart! I have overcome the world*" John 16:33 NIV. He has provided little reminders in my life that I will be okay: parents and in-laws that love and support us, friends that celebrate and mourn with us, a dog that is objectively the cutest and the best, a cozy home over our heads, family through relationship that doesn't leave our side. And those are enough to get me through, to remind that

everything is okay and it will continue to be okay.

This is a sacred space where your reflections,
pain, grief and joys are held with grace

_____
_____
_____
_____
_____
_____
_____
_____
_____
_____
_____
_____
_____
_____
_____
_____
_____
_____
_____

Sometimes #5

Sometimes I Feel Like Healthcare Professionals Suck

Sometimes I feel like no one in the health care setting cares, and I say this as someone who works in the health care setting.

I am an occupational therapist, so I've been on the other side. I've had the patient in my room, crying, holding my hand, asking for hope and answers. And while I'm not perfect, I try my best to give it to them. At the very least, every human deserves to be listened to, to experience some semblance of genuine empathy. I don't remember that happening with either of my losses, with either of my surgeries, with my initial appointments with fertility specialists.

You are in one of the most vulnerable states going through just the process of pregnancy itself. You recognize millions of women have done this before you, but YOU haven't yet. So, you rely on those professionals, the ones who have seen this a hundred times before and went to years upon years of schooling to tell you exactly what to do so you and your baby are safe and healthy. And then the worst happens, you have bleeding, you have cramping, your HCG labs aren't rising like they should. But instead of answers, you get nothing, maybe some pity. The front office sees you choking back sobs as you wait in the check in line to try to get an emergency appointment last minute, and they don't even offer a tissue much less some empathy.

I remember going in for my second D&C, the doctor was running behind. Already a nervous wreck, and three hours of distracting YouTube videos later, I hit my call bell. In summary: Nurse, what is going on here? I think I'm being a pretty patient patient. "Oh you're waiting on Dr. So and So, well he's an OB so he's probably stuck delivering a baby!" Lady, excuse me? Do you not see the diagnosis on my chart? My ice-cold stare hits her completely unaware face.

We go in for the results of the second D&C. Surely this will provide some answers. Perhaps there is something that comes up genetically with the baby that will give us some closure. The doctor comes in and calmly explains to us that they put the baby in the wrong formula and therefore were unable to complete testing. He goes on to say that unfortunately I am a statistic and there is nothing to show why I am experiencing the worst tragedies of my life. I am silently hoping that it is the worst tragedy I ever have to experience in my entirety. That's it. It feels like a "Thanks for playing the pregnancy game, but you did not win this round. Do not pass go, do not collect $200, do not pick up your baby on the way out."

You may have similar experiences. You may be able to relate. And if that is the case my sincerest apologies because health care professionals should be better. They should be the ones that see you hurting through possibly one of the worst hurts of your life, and they should care. But healthcare professionals are also human, and therefore they will disappoint you as well.

I am embarking on a new health care journey. I have a new Ob/Gyn I am seeing that came from a referral from a friend as well as a functional medicine clinic, also a friendly referral. The jury is still out, and I can only hope that you have found medical professionals that care and can provide you answers.

Now, a quick shoutout to the ER tech who did my intake when I first walked in with blood-soaked pants and a blanket sheepishly wrapped around me as I had come straight from work. She demanded to staff that I have a private room, and she shared that she had been through this before. I appreciated that demonstration of vulnerability and kindness. And another shoutout to the ER doctor who gently confirmed I had experienced my first incomplete miscarriage. She was kind in her delivery of such disturbing news, and she shared her story of two consecutive losses and being told she would never deliver a biological child and now has two healthy children. She told me not to give up hope, and I continue to think of her. Last shoutout to my therapist, who pushes me through the silences, who listens without judgement, and who helps me strategize coping so that I do not completely give in to despair. So sometimes I feel like those healthcare professionals most definitely do not suck.

This is a sacred space where your reflections, pain, grief and joys are held with grace

_____
_____
_____
_____
_____
_____
_____
_____
_____
_____
_____
_____
_____
_____
_____
_____
_____
_____

Sometimes #6

Sometimes I Feel Like God Hates Me

Sometimes I feel like God literally couldn't care less about me.

I shout and scream *Where are you?* This feels like a punishment, or at the very least he has abandoned me. It is too difficult to grasp how God could let this happen. I don't deserve two losses, two babies in heaven and not on earth, two surgeries, two terrible experiences where I watched blood gush from me and felt labor pains and sat there silently crying for hours. How could God ever let anyone hear the words "*There is no heartbeat?*"

And it doesn't stop there, there are triggers and reminders everywhere. I made my dentist appointment when I was pregnant, they ask me when I'm there to confirm that I am indeed still pregnant. NO! I'm not pregnant. Oh did you have your baby? No. God, you couldn't have side barred that conversation? My apps keep sending me updates on how much my baby should and would be growing. God you couldn't have stopped that email from coming through today, or changed my Pinterest algorithm to stop advertising nursery themes, or not put an 8-month pregnant women in front of me in the coffee line?

Patients at work are endlessly asking me if I have kids and if not, how come? People, learn some damn manners. And once again, I'm questioning why God didn't inspire a different conversation topic in their minds. I numb myself with TV and all the sudden my favorite character is pregnant. Would have been nice if you inspired me to watch a different show, God. I blame him for everything because I've been told he controls everything.

I call out to God and wait for the love and peace and comfort to reverberate back. All I hear is my own sorry echo. It mocks me and only fuels my new bold belief that God is gone. He is out helping the orphans of the world, the starving families, the war in another country, but not me. Me, he has abandoned. Me, he does not care about. Me, he must hate. Because how could I feel so crippled, so lost, so devastated, and get silence back from my God? It pierces my soul. It shakes my faith.

All my mishaps throughout the day, I stare up at God in anger. Really? You couldn't have stopped that one? I throw my phone in frustration, it cracks, there's $200 we really can't afford to not have. My husband's workload has doubled and is overwhelming and stressful to the point that he is unable to fully be there for me. Didn't want to postpone that season God?

Let's just have it hit all at once instead. They offer to do testing on my second baby at my D&C procedure. At our follow up, they have put the baby in the wrong formula, and they were unable to test. God, you're kidding right? I blame it all on God because it's easiest. If he is all powerful, then he can handle all my frustration.

The list is endless, and in my mind, that means God hates me. He has abandoned me. All these things that I believe He is powerful enough to change, and instead he lets me endure the agonizing misery of it all. For the first time in my life I think to myself

"This God is no God of mine."

This is a sacred space where your reflections,

pain, grief and joys are held with grace

_____

_____

_____

_____

_____

_____

_____

_____

_____

_____

_____

_____

_____

_____

_____

_____

_____

_____

_____

Sometimes #7

Sometimes I Want to Tell Everyone to F#@! Off

Sometimes, I think I could murder everyone around me.

We all know the hurtful statements. They're cited in every book I read, in every post I see, in every video I watch. The seemingly well-intentioned but unfortunately well debilitating remarks come in all shapes and sizes, but what can be the most difficult is who they are coming from. From parents, from friends, from spouses, from strangers. Each perspective holds a special kind of dagger all its own.

When it comes

> From a *parent...*I think, aren't you supposed to know me better? Aren't you supposed to make me feel better?
> From a *friend...* Just shut up and be there for me! Don't say these hurtful things.
> From a *spouse...* You can't relate! Your body didn't go through what mine did.
> From a *stranger...* You don't even know me or my story. Stop talking!

Everyone just fu** off! I scream in my head, sometimes into a pillow. Maybe you can relate to these responses rolling around in your mind, or perhaps you even said them aloud. You won't find judgment here.

Everyone is annoying, no one understands, and yet everyone typically has something to say. Or on the other hand, they say nothing at all like it didn't even happen. Sometimes it's the suggestions. "Well my mom did this... My doctor had me do this... I got another opinion... You husband needs to do... You need to try..." The opinions and options and recommendations are overwhelming at best, suffocating at worst. Did I ask for them? Everyone back off!

And then the comments we all dread hearing but all typically hear at some point:

> *This is so common.*
> *There was probably something wrong with that one, it had all the bad genes.*
> *You can always try again.*
> *You can always adopt.*
> *Maybe stop trying for a little bit.*
> *You have to trust God's timing and plan.*

It's funny though how, on the second time around, these comments don't hold the same weight. I want to look at all the faces behind these words and say well now I'm less than 1% of women, so is it that common? Did both my babies have "bad genes?" Should I just keep trying again and miscarrying? How about you stop having sex and thinking about your all consuming desire? God's timing and plan sucks.

Angry much, Alex? I. Am. Livid. An emotion I'm not very familiar with. My patience is now razor thin. Watch out world, you are all skating on thin ice in my mind. In fact, that ice is cracked and there's already holes of "F You" in it so most likely you're falling into one of those at some point. My insides are raging, and nothing is quenching them. It's a fire of engrossing defeat, frustration, and misery, and it's easiest and best taken out on others. It's more destructive that way.

And what angers me most and what cripples me most, is my anger at God. God, what the hell? It's on the tip of my tongue God F off. He would still love me through it...He can handle it. I could say it and still be forgiven. But his nearness stops me. Because I know this rush of anger and outward expression of distress will pass. He, once again, is carrying me through this as I kick and scream and pound away on his back. He sings and soothes and pats me on my back till eventually I release that anger.

For a brief moment, I remember what it's like to not hate the world.

This is a sacred space where your reflections,
pain, grief and joys are held with grace

_____
_____
_____
_____
_____
_____
_____
_____
_____
_____
_____
_____
_____
_____
_____
_____
_____
_____

Sometimes #8

Sometimes I Think I'll Never Have a Biological Child

I get my period again, and it absolutely sucks.

My heart is broken, my dreams are shattered. I hear that voice again, you will never have another pregnancy and you will not have a biological child. What possible timing could God be waiting for? Month after month, I face the death of my deepest hopes and desires. That's what gets me, that's what is so hard. That each month I face disappointment. It's not just one huge, colossal disappointment that you wade through. It's continued disappointment, month after month. A huge, smack-you-in-the-face, punch-you-in-the-gut disappointment that stares at you from freaking toilet paper, as if it couldn't get be more degrading and embarrassing and shameful.

It's a wave. And each month, hope wells up. It is the force that is so strong behind the eventual wave that hits some odd 28 days later. You're drowning and choking and coughing up disappointment, and when you feel you finally can come up from air, another damn wave hits you. The cycle repeats itself. Have you ever seen those big wave contests? I imagine myself a speck on my board at the base of the wave. I am staring at this colossal force of nature headed my way, and I feel myself still. There is nothing I can do to change it or avoid it or swim through it. I just have to stay there and take this beating. I have tried to change, avoid, and swim, and it doesn't get me far. You may or may not initially feel the pounding wave with those tactics, but the avoidance is only temporary.

I have found it is best to ride it, to let it take me. It will not kill me. This wave will leave me battered and bruised and heartsick, but when I get through it, I can start to hope again. I have weeks where I can try to cough all that disappointment out and start to breathe in the faint spray of hope. That is what I will cling to. That is the only thing I can cling to in this sea I find myself in.

We would also love to adopt and foster children. That's always been on the table for my husband and me. We talked about it when dating, when we first married. But we had it planned. Biological child first, maybe twins? They run in the family you know! Then adoption, then fostering, maybe sprinkle in another biological child along the way. But you know what my mistake was right there? We had it planned. I'm learning planning is not bad, but planning

31

is not fact, and that is a hard lesson to learn. Now I'm at the point where I don't even plan, but I question God's plan all the time. Mostly I just want to know God's plan, anything, even a peek. But I guess we don't get to see behind the curtain. Because if we did, I don't think we would sign up for God's plan.

I don't think I would sign up for the heartbreak to get to the beauty of what my life, of what my children and family, will eventually be.

This is a sacred space where your reflections,
pain, grief and joys are held with grace

_____
_____
_____
_____
_____
_____
_____
_____
_____
_____
_____
_____
_____
_____
_____
_____
_____
_____

Sometimes #1

Sometimes I Feel Like I Can't Get Out of Bed... Or Off the Couch

Sometimes I lie there willing my legs to move.

Just turn over onto your side, I tell myself. That's the first step to getting out of bed. But they don't do it. Something has happened to the connection between my brain and my legs, it's not firing. I'm pleading my body to move, but at the same time I'm wondering what the point is. I miss waking up and not moving because I was so sublimely happy I was pregnant. But that is gone, it's been taken from me twice now. I imagine God picking me up from under my armpits and then my legs are just dragging across the floor. He drags me into the kitchen, where it takes me 20 minutes to get a glass out and take a sip of water. Sometimes he drags me to the couch, sometimes I don't make it there. Instead, I'm stuck sitting on the kitchen floor. How long have I been here? I start to wonder. Silent tears have been consistently falling for some time now.

These are the dark days. They're mostly numb with some intense grief sprinkled in there. That's what I am now, a very bland, meager soup. You take some base stock of numbness, and sprinkle in all consuming grief, a dash of bitterness, and stir in some exhaustion. There you go, serve me up. I'm not delicious but you have to drink all of me because well, there's no other choice.

These days are not every day but they very much exist. They are poop, there's no other way around it. These are the days I'm mourning and grieving the loss of the life I once expected to live. A life with no infertility, with no pregnancy loss, with people that I could always relate to, but that is not the life for me. I think of the Disney song "Yo Ho a Pirate's Life For Me," I change the words. Yo Ho a Depressing Life For Me! I am facing the death of the life I thought I had, and if I'm being honest, the life I thought I deserved. RIP to my picture-perfect planned life.

Ok, I'm in the bed or I'm on the kitchen floor or I'm on the couch, how do I move on next? I picture myself walking into the bathroom, I can almost feel myself brushing my hair, I can see my clothes I pick out for work, but then I'm brought back to reality and none of that has happened. Dang it, I'm still on the couch. And that's when I give it to God. Clearly, I'm not doing that great of a job getting my life together, of trying to get through the day. So he has to make me move, he keeps nudging me into each room, into each next task, because that's all I can focus on.

I get one thing done at a time, sometimes that means just breathing.

I take a breath in, inhale, I take a breath out, exhale.

One step forward, *I did it.*

And for now, that's all I need to do.

This is a sacred space where your reflections, pain, grief and joys are held with grace

---

Sometimes #10

Sometimes I Feel Like I Have the Best Husband in the World

My husband is my absolute foundation, my rock, and I am his.

We have an ebb and flow, he falls apart and I'm there. I fall apart, and he's there. When we both fall apart, we just hold each other tightly till one of us finds supernatural strength from Jesus.

We have a tense argument mostly spurred from our aching hearts, and he sits on the dining room chair, silent. No words, no looks, hardly any blinking. Just quiet tears slipping down his face. My heart breaks, and at that moment, I want nothing more in the world than to stop those numb tears. But I can't stop them, I can't do anything or say anything to change them. So instead, I'm just near. I sit at his feet, I hug his calf, I kiss his knee. Because there is nothing to say or do. I have felt what he feels, and unfortunately, I know the feeling all too well. Well enough to know there is nothing to be done.

I come home from a baby shower, despondent, wailing on our bed. I can't move, I can hardly breathe, I can only cry. I try to speak, and it comes out garbled and ugly. My husband lays there too. He holds me, sometimes he squeezes me. But most importantly he's just there. Occasionally we offer each other muffled I love you's because what else is there to say? He tells me it's unfair I'm going through this. He tells me we will be parents one day. He tells me he's sorry it's happening this way. I tell him I'd take a life of misery with him than a life of perfection without him.

We are forming a new chapter with each other where we rely on one another more than we ever have before.

In a world where I feel I have no one who can relate to me in the moment, he can a bit. Not in the same way physically, and not completely in the same way emotionally. But we share a loss and grief so intimate and intense, our souls are bound. When I feel my legs giving out on me, when I feel I can't suck in enough oxygen, he's there. He's there carrying me, he's there telling me to breathe. He's there showing me God's unconditional and unending love, even when he doesn't know it. Sometimes I take that for granted, but other times it's so clear to me. My husband is showing me the picture-perfect love of God here on earth.

I try to remember our happy times together as well, like when I first told him I was pregnant, and attempted filming his response. He was in a towel fresh out of the shower, and he stops wearing the towel... *Guess we're not showing that one to the family.* I remember the second time I told him I was pregnant, and I was so nervous but he was so happy and full of joyful tears and remained hopeful when I couldn't. I remember at 9 weeks, showing him a physical representation of how small our baby's feet were. I exclaim, "*They're this small!*" My fingertips form the smallest dot. We look into each other's eyes in wonder and excitement and joy.

I miss sharing those feelings together. I miss those feelings, period. But it's good to remember the moments on the mountaintop when you're in the valley. It reminds me we will experience the mountaintop again.

He drives me to baby showers. He works longer and harder so I can work less and hardly. He prays for me even when he's mad at God and doubting his very existence. My husband is my firm foundation, and when I'm strong enough, I am his. We set time aside weekly, if not daily, to talk about how sad we are we lost our two babies. We talk about how it permeates every aspect of our lives, friendships, work, pervasive thoughts, family relationships, our every day to day. We get each other. We may process and grieve differently but we do it together. Us against the world, kid. I look into his eyes, into his soul. There's sadness, there's determination, there's hope and hopelessness side by side.

I look into his eyes. We can do this.

This is a sacred space where your reflections,
pain, grief and joys are held with grace

_____
_____
_____
_____
_____
_____
_____
_____
_____
_____
_____
_____
_____
_____
_____
_____
_____
_____
_____
_____

Sometimes #11

Sometimes I Feel Like Pregnancy is a Miracle and I'm Happy for Others

But honestly and sadly, I don't feel this way most days.

I'm hoping for it to become more frequent, though. Now, I say it's not most days because it's not strictly this feeling most days. Most days, I have happy mixed with envy, I have in-awe sprinkled with bitter, I have excitement with jealousy. Rarely, is it pure happiness and belief in the true miracle of pregnancy. But on those days that I do, it is a sweet feeling. It is a reminder that God is incredible.

I do believe in being there for my friends, and I want to physically show that. I am happy for them, I am excited for them, I am there for them too. I have yet to say no to a baby shower. Now, that move isn't for everyone. I completely respect every women's decision in that regard because I get it, it's not an easy one. And frankly, some of those close to me would tell you I made a mistake going but hey it's my decision to make.

I see my friend's baby bumps, their glowing smiles, talking about their baby moving, picking out names. What a joy! What a beautiful, happy time in their lives that they absolutely deserve. I see women in all circumstances pregnant around me as I go about life, and I marvel at the miracle of this shared connection. The amount of hormones and timing and genetics that have to be absolutely perfect to have a baby is actually staggering when you think about it. I had a doctor compare it to when they launch the shuttles near me from Cape Canaveral. He said the amount that has to be absolutely precise and has to 100% go right to get that shuttle to go off safely and perfectly is similar to the sperm meeting the egg and producing a healthy baby to full term. But that's how effective our bodies are made to be.

I ask my friends questions about their nursery decorations, breast pumps, and pregnancy pains. I listen genuinely and intently. I want to hear their unique experiences. And when it's not going so perfectly or they're frustrated, I am able to listen to their vents and challenges. Now again let me repeat, it is not often I have on rose colored glasses without mixed emotions. But some days it's pure and it exists, and I am very grateful for those days. Because I deeply cherish and love my friends.

My mom consistently tells me that the beautiful, spiritual friends I have are once in a lifetime. They have been my rock, and I hope at times, they have felt I can be theirs. We share tears together over my frustrations with infertility, and in the same visit, share laughs about their baby's silly poses on an ultrasound. We hold hands and mourn my losses, and then talk about their wait times at OB appointments and which doctors they hope will be on call for delivery. The dichotomy is deep and intimate but allows the truest most genuine friendships I could hope for.

I am happy for their joys and their future family. And when these babies arrive, I will be here with open arms to help and love and support. I want better than the best for these beautiful women because they deserve it.

And I want them to know how incredibly grateful I am for them and for the miracles growing in their bodies.

This is a sacred space where your reflections, pain, grief and joys are held with grace

_____

_____

_____

_____

_____

_____

_____

_____

_____

_____

_____

_____

_____

_____

_____

_____

_____

_____

Sometimes #12

Sometimes I Want to Hug The Women
Who Have Shared Their Stories

Sometimes I think of all the women who have shared that they've suffered the same at some point in their lives, and my jaw drops.

How can something so heart breaking and earth-shattering affect 1 in 4 women? How do all these women have a dismal membership in this crummy club? But I'm so incredibly grateful for the women who have shared their stories with me. The ER tech, the ER doctor, my family members, my close friends, my friends of friends, family friends. You are strong, bada$$ women! I may not be able to relate to all of them or all their situations, and they may not be able to completely relate to me but we share a bond. We share an understanding of an unimaginable grief.

In my mind, I hug each of them, and in some instances, in reality. Whether they're ready for it or not, I'm coming in with a hug. I feel their pain. I feel their triumph on good days. I feel their anxious excitement if and when they get news of a rainbow baby. I embrace their beautiful vulnerability in sharing possibly the greatest heartbreak of their life. And I honor and remember their loss. I think that is one of the most unique parts of everyone's pregnancy and infant loss stories.

How do you remember and honor that life within your life?

Some may choose to honor and not remember. Some may be silent in their goodbyes. Some may host an intimate memorial service, or even do a small birthday celebration every year. Everyone is different and that is okay. I think the point is doing something because it provides a connection to a truly pivotal moment in one's life. We found two small butterfly tokens we hung with fishing line in our front yard tree. I close them in the palm of my hand when I need to feel closure. On our first due date, I sent out a text to family and close friends, asking them to send a prayer up to our little one saying they were missed and loved, and I plan on doing the same on our second due date. Everyone's story is different. I've seen people performs acts of gratitude on due dates, have wind chimes in remembrance, place their baby's ashes in a special box or spread them. All of these are so heartbreakingly beautiful and perfect for each person. I honor and respect them and give them the biggest hug.

Support groups for this kind of grief are hard to come by. It's not your typical grief, and for whatever reason, there's not a lot of physical meet up opportunities. Thank goodness for the internet. Now I've said before, social media, specifically Facebook for me, was like walking a minefield. Typically, I stepped on something that blew up my day so I stopped going there. But a friend of mine suggested Tik Tok, and *surprisingly* I found my support group there.

I started following four women who were genuine and broken and hopeful and inspiring in their fertility journeys. Three had experienced loss, much too frequently, and gave me a story to relate to, a metaphysical shoulder to cry on. I occasionally comment on their posts and give them hugs from afar. I hurt for them, but I am incredibly grateful for their candor and for finding a group of ladies that sadly gets it without me having to explain it. I hope you find that; I hope you have that.

And I hope outside of this book, you have something that helps remind you,

you are not alone.

This is a sacred space where your reflections, pain, grief and joys are held with grace

_____
_____
_____
_____
_____
_____
_____
_____
_____
_____
_____
_____
_____
_____
_____
_____
_____
_____

Sometimes #13

Sometimes I Feel Strong

Sometimes I feel strong. Sometimes I listen to worship music.

I get done listening to "Promises" by Maverick City Music, and I feel invincible. I feel God has made me invincible. Not that storms won't come, the exact opposite in fact - I'm in the middle of said storm, but that it won't knock me down beyond recovery, that it won't drown me, that it won't take away my joy, my faith, and my life. I feel badass. *Should I use that word?* I don't know, that's the best way I can say it. I look at what God has gotten me through. The year prior my doctor thought I had cancer. I was going through testing and ER visits and unmet pain. Tears and absolute fear for almost two months, but I ended up on the other side healthy and ready to keep living and thriving. Now this year and a half, I suffer through infertility, through the loss of my two precious babies, through the frustration watching seven friends at this point announce their pregnancy while I go to seven doctor's appointments and blood draws a month. But I can do it because God CAN do it.

"*I can do all things through him who gives me strength.*" (Philippians 4:13 NIV).

I know you have your own story of health struggles, of relationship struggles, and if you're reading this book, some type of fertility and pregnancy loss struggle. You can relate!

I feel Him preparing me for a strength that others don't get the chance to build. My husband and I build a foundation of faith and stability and endurance that I never imagined happening. And how much more will that strengthen us as individuals, as spouses, and ultimately as parents? Wouldn't any parent do absolutely anything for the betterment of their child? During the moments I feel strong, I have this perspective. I am enduring ANYTHING for the betterment of raising my children with wisdom, with perseverance, with unconditional love. I have that perspective when I think of my babies that I lost. All things good come from God (James 1:17), so follow me here.

If all good things come from God, I'm believing these awful things come from a place of evil, of sin, and ultimately not of God. If God's plan was to not have these babies here on earth, to me, that spells out that their life would not have been from God, it would not have been good. There may have been grave suffering, there may have been intense pain (which we all already experience here on earth), but to even a greater degree that I or my children could truly handle. So again, as a parent, wouldn't I sacrifice my happiness and my desire to have them here on earth so that they could live beautiful, peaceful, perfect lives in heaven from the start of their small precious lives?

You may not get here, you may not feel that way. Let me make something very clear, THAT IS OKAY. The above statements have been the absolute hardest things for me to wade through and wrestle with, but coming on the other side of them and having this revolution has been empowering and uplifting for me. That may not be the case for you. If that makes you more frustrated and more angry, let me say it again, THAT IS OKAY. Everyone processes differently, and that means everyone's strength looks different for everyone. But I found this to be a comforting thought that offered strength in a universal sense: You are a mother, you are a father, you are a parent. Your child may not be here on earth but you imagined that child's life when you got the positive test. You became a parent when you found out you had a baby growing inside you and imagined feeling their first kicks in your belly, their birth, planning their first birthday, days of skipping school to have a mommy daughter day, first boyfriends or girlfriends, all the above. You experienced glimpses of your life with them, and then had all that ripped away and had to switch gears to planning their memorial service perhaps, their loss, delivery via surgery or at home. No more belly kicks, but more likely contractions with none of the result. If you can get through that, you are strong. You may not feel strong, and I know I didn't. But I look back and said I went through that?! God, you carried me through that? How can I not believe God is carrying me through the weakest time in my life only to leave me stronger on the other side? I look at what I'm growing through, and think I'm still alive and breathing? Hell yes, I'm freaking strong. In fact, I'm amazing! And so are you. You are amazing and amazingly loved.

So today I feel strong. Today I feel like there is a purpose and plan that is beyond difficult and challenging, but God has given me the supernatural strength to persevere and hope for better. I recognize and remember our pain, but I have the glimpse of a whole picture where I am burned to be beautiful, lovely, righteous, holy. Another Maverick City Music shoutout. If you haven't already, I highly recommend you give them a listen. I keep fighting the good fight, maybe because I have no other choice, but also because this strength I am gaining just keeps surmounting. And that snowball of strength, gaining momentum, is preparing me to be the wise woman God has called me to be, including the best parent I can be. I keep coming back to this verse.

"Not only so, but we also glory in our sufferings, because we know that suffering produces perseverance; perseverance, character; and character, hope. And hope does not put us to shame, because God's love has been poured out into our hearts through the Holy Spirit, who has been given to us" Romans 5:3 NIV.

This is a sacred space where your reflections,
pain, grief and joys are held with grace

_____
_____
_____
_____
_____
_____
_____
_____
_____
_____
_____
_____
_____
_____
_____
_____
_____
_____
_____
_____

Sometimes #14

Sometimes I Know God is Good and I Will Get Through This

This one is hard to get to, and I don't feel it every day.

The days I do feel it and know it are good. They're full of contentment and promise and peace. I didn't say they're full of joy and happiness and no struggle. No, we're not there yet. Sometimes I wonder if my life and if my days will forever be tinged with a little sadness. That thought does not daunt me today though. I take it for what it is. Maybe there will always be a little sadness in my life. Happiness, or even my deeper joy, may be painted with the faintest overcoat of blue, of someone who has lived through heartache and hope and the worst that this life has to offer and lived to tell the tale. I'm okay with that. It gives me complexity. I experience a richer and fuller version of life. And most importantly, I viscerally experience God's goodness and love and never-ending nearness (Psalm 139:3).

He is good, he loves me, and he hurts when I hurt. Some days I feel this clearly, but every day I know this. Even if that knowledge is buried under heaps of doubt, it's there, and it's not going away. I say it a little louder and with a little more confidence. I know God is good and I will get through this. This life on earth will take you and beat you, chew you up and spit you out. But I know my God won't, and I know that he'll carry me and you and our loved ones and our babies when we can't. He will love you and me and the precious lives we lost more than we can imagine. "Neither height nor depth, nor anything else in all creation, will be able to separate us from the love of God that is in Christ Jesus our Lord." (Romans 8:39 NIV). That means my doubt, my frustration, my floundering through this life, cannot separate me from God's love or from God's plan for me.

I don't know what that plan looks like yet, but I know when I'm holding my future (God fill in the blank here), I will be perfectly happy and content. I will say, this is what my heart was yearning for. That does not take away from the sadness of losing my two pregnancies this year, nor does it remove my longing for having them come to term and being here with little ones right now. But it gives me a hope that my desire for a family will take shape with God's guidance someway and somehow on earth, and that in heaven, I will find my complete family. I will feel whole.

So, I give it all to God, my heart, my dreams, my desires. You can have it all God because you can do something better with it than I can. But I must truly believe that in order to give up what is so precious to me. Was it ever really mine to begin with? Sometimes that's a hard thought to grapple with. I tell myself and I tell God, I'm going to wait on you. I've tasted your goodness, I trust in your promise... another shout out to Maverick City Music. I can wait because God gives me the strength to wait. It does not come from others, from this world, and it most certainly does not come from me. He is my never ending well of listening, encouragement, strength, and restoration. That's what we are in the process of, being restored. And let me tell you, it's not easy work. It's hard and gritty and sometimes feels never ending. It can be the definition of long suffering. But it is soul strengthening, thirst quenching work, and I know that it gives me a foundation to take on anything that this sometimes crummy world will offer.

God is good, he is so, so good. I hope you have days where you feel that, where you are confident that you will get through this. That, yes, he gave you more than you can handle, but so that you could throw that burden on him because he is the ONLY one that can handle it. Not you, not your spouse, not your parent, not your best friend, not your counselor. But God can, and even more than that, he wants to. He wants to be there for his children, and pull them through and eventually out of their misery.

So, I let him. Take it away, God. It's your show now, not mine. I don't want to star in this dark comedy anymore, time for you to take the lead. I get to a point where I am more than fine being a supportive character. And I can feel my hope building, I can feel my resolve growing, and I know my future is coming to fruition. This is part of it! This journey is part of my future. It's not all the outcome, it's my process getting there, that will ultimately help shape me as a mom, a wife, a woman, a human. It's happening for you too, and girl, I hope you feel that somedays. I hope you can recognize the good days. And I hope and know that at some point we will have more of these good days than bad days. Even on those dark, dark, break-me-down days, my little truth teller in my mind speaks,

God is good. You will get through this.

This is a sacred space where your reflections,
pain, grief and joys are held with grace

_____
_____
_____
_____
_____
_____
_____
_____
_____
_____
_____
_____
_____
_____
_____
_____
_____
_____
_____

Afterword

Wading in the Aftermath

There's something you may have noticed while reading these chapters...

Most of the positive chapters have a bible verse in them, and most of the positive chapters hold more words. I noticed that halfway through writing this. I found that interesting, and I think it goes to show on the good days, I am aware of God's presence. In addition, I want positivity and good days to be more frequent. I want those passages longer because that's how I want to feel the majority of the time. On the good days, I cling to Jesus, I read the word, and I welcome God into my heart to create the peace and comfort I cannot. On the bad days, there are no bible verses. There are no bible verses because there's nothing in the bible to back up those dark, harsh, hurting thoughts. There's nothing that supports truth in those.

That doesn't mean God isn't there. He hasn't abandoned me, he's still right there. Not only is he holding my hand, sometimes he is literally holding my body to get me through the day. I'm just not aware of that presence. He's waiting for the invite, he wants that to be our decision. I can choose to be aware of God's help or I can allow my focus to settle into what the enemy says is true: God is not there, God does not care, God is punishing me, and I, as a human, have a better plan. I think that is the undercurrent in all my negative days. Those days will undeniably happen, and that is because we are human. But if we can recognize that they are lies and they exist because we are human and not perfect, then hopefully we can see that this tragedy in our life also represents the lie of eternal negativity here on earth. Our true glory and reconciliation with God is in heaven. It is not on this earth. We get glimpses of it here on earth, but this is not meant to be our forever home and therefore we are not meant to desire to be here forever. I type these words and they may have an air of confidence, but let me be frank. That thought is all of the following: scary, frustrating, relieving, daunting, inspiring, and therefore something I continue to wrestle with and through.

You may have been gifted this book, and you may not be overly spiritual or filled with faith. That is okay. I hope you still find this book relatable, and you still experience the ultimate goal for why I wrote this book - you are NOT alone. You can feel angry and happy at the same time, or you can feel persistent sadness for two weeks and then find yourself belly laughing for the first time one morning. There are no linear timelines to process through an experience like ours. It yo-yo's back and forth, it swings wildly up and staggeringly down like a pendulum but the goal is to feel all of it. Because when you don't, it festers and stays deep inside and starts to eat away at that parts that truly make you you. And you are amazing and amazingly loved, remember?

I wrote 14 "*Sometimes I Feel...*" because it truly felt like I was experiencing 2 weeks worth of emotions in a day, sometimes even an hour. If you don't feel all of these emotions, guess what? That is okay! Sometimes talking to others, I realized I didn't feel what they felt or I felt what they were feeling but much more or less intensely. This disconnect is natural and normal, we are all individuals. No experience is the same, but I do believe there is an undercurrent of connectivity and relation that allows for a shared but not identical experience. I am here for you, I pray for you, I get you. I remember my husband in our darkest days saying none of our friends "get us." The books, the friends, the family, they weren't walking the same path by our side. I'm here to say that I am, or at the very least these words are, walking the same exact path as you are right now. I get it, and I don't know what comes next or how to make it happen. And more importantly, God is right there by you. A lot of sermons, songs, and Bible verses, point to the fact that God sent Jesus to earth to experience all of the faults of humanhood. He experienced temptation (Matthew 4:1-11), betrayal (Mark 14:18), death of loved ones (John 11:33-36), and received the answer "no" to his deepest plea to God (Matthew 26:38-46) so he could relate to us. But sometimes I wonder did he experience the loss of a pregnancy? Did he experience not knowing what his future family looks like? How can he relate to that one? To be honest, that's a question I have on my list for when I get to heaven. But the further I dwell in that thought, the more I came to the conclusion that God did experience the loss of his son Jesus Christ. He actually willingly allowed him to experience pain, torture, and temporary death. And who did he do that for? Me! My husband! My babies! You and your babes! (John 3:16). And he is waiting on the verdict of his future family. He waits while freewill allows us to make the decision to be apart from God's family. He doesn't make that decision for us, although he so desperately wants that for him and for us. So, in conclusion I think he has an idea. Although I'm still skeptical on the exact comparison.

I'm writing after another month of negative pregnancy tests, another month of more baby showers and pregnancy announcements that aren't mine, and another month, where I so desperately cling to the hope of Jesus. My future is unknown, and some days I handle that well and with grace, and other days that thought completely wrecks me, and it's hard to know how I'll cope in the next few hours or even tomorrow. But the good news is, I don't have to know what tomorrow looks like.

""Therefore, do not worry about tomorrow, for tomorrow will worry about itself. Each day has enough trouble of its own." (Matthew 6:34 NIV.

I make progress, and then fall back 5 steps. I'm learning and growing and crying and screaming all at once. If you're there, I'm there with you. Hang in there. I'm loving you from afar and through these words, and most importantly,

God is loving you.
He loves you all the time.
He loves you when you don't or can't love him back.
And he loves you no matter where you're at in this crazy rollercoaster of a journey.

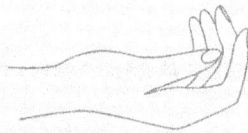

Ways to help those experiencing infertility
A guide for the well-intended

Grief-Appropriate Phrases to Say

- *"I'm so sorry for your loss/your struggle. I'm here for you, however you need me to be."*
- *"No need to respond. I just wanted to let you know I'm thinking of you and here if you need anything."*
- *"You don't need to be strong during this time. Your loss is very real and very deep."*
- *"Would you like to talk about how you're grieving with... (loss, infertility, etc)?"* **Even months later!**
- *"How is your partner/spouse doing with everything?"* Husbands hurt, too.
- *"Can I pray for you and your baby and your partner?"* (If they're religious)
- And particularly for those that haven't experienced this situation: *"I have no idea what you're going through or what this feels like, and I am so sorry that this happened."*

Grief-Appropriate Actions to Express Care

- Drop off food, a favorite snack, or a grubhub gift card. Even a grocery store gift card can be particularly helpful, especially if their loved one isn't working.
- Providing a small care package - lotion, cozy socks, hair mask *(post partum hair loss is real...)*, comfy blanket, or hydration packets
- Gifting special mementos, such as donations to charity in honor of the baby, memorable Christmas ornaments, jewelry, special pictures (check out Etsy), flowers or plants
- Provide them this book as a resource

additional resources for those experiencing grief arising from miscarriage and infertility

1) In-person resource support groups in one's area

2) Online resource support groups, such as Facebook communities

3) Books

- *Held* - Abbey Wedgeworth,
- *Loved Baby* - Sarah Philpott,
- *It Not Supposed to Be This Way* - Lysa TerKeurst.

4) Music

- Maverick City Music Spotify playlist (the songs *I'm Going to Wait on You*, *Jireh*, and *Promises* particularly have and will continue to get me through my best and worst moments)

5) Digital Media- such as grief-centered podcasts and Youtube channels

6) Grief Therapy- it is completely OK to seek clinical support from a trusted provider during the emotional, physical, mental, and spiritual roller coaster that is infertility.

In addition to these resources, if you are looking to vent or need someone to listen, I'm here as much as I can be. Please reach me at this email address if you'd like to share your story or have any questions regarding my experience of infertility and recurrent miscarriage:

miscarriageconversations@gmail.com

additional space for notes, cries, lamentations, references, memories and optimism

_____

_____

_____

_____

_____

_____

_____

_____

_____

_____

_____

_____

_____

_____

_____

_____

_____

A.L. MARSTON

about the author
A.L. MARSTON

A.L. Marston's passions for writing and helping others began at an early age. Born and raised in sunny Florida, she finds inspiration and solace in nature and the beach, and is daily surrounded by the love of the family and friends in her hometown. Marston studied at the University of Florida, where she received both her bachelors and masters degrees.

Marston and her husband, after getting married in 2019, did not expect to find such difficulty in their attempts to conceive, but found ways to persevere through their faith and their mutual support of each other - and through a lot of unconditional love from their sweet puppy. And In 2023, Marston gave birth to her daughter 12 weeks early after a complicated conception, pregnancy, and birth experience.

Each day, both in and outside of her vocation as an occupational therapist, Marston cherishes each day God has given her and hopes to be a light to others.